STICKER and COLOUR-IN P|

OLD MacDONALD'S FARM

ILLUSTRATED BY
JENNY TULIP

Old MacDonald had a farm
Ee-Yi-Ee-Yi-O!
And on that farm he had some Ducks
Ee-Yi-Ee-Yi-O!
With a QUACK QUACK here

And a QUACK QUACK there
Here a QUACK
There a QUACK
Everywhere a QUACK QUACK
Old MacDonald had a farm
Ee-Yi-Ee-Yi-O!

Old MacDonald had a farm
Ee-Yi-Ee-Yi-O!
And on that farm he had some Pigs
Ee-Yi-Ee-Yi-O!
With a HONK HONK here

And a HONK HONK there
Here a HONK
There a HONK
Everywhere a HONK HONK
Old MacDonald had a farm
Ee-Yi-Ee-Yi-O!

Old MacDonald had a farm
Ee-Yi-Ee-Yi-O!
And on that farm he had some Sheep
Ee-Yi-Ee-Yi-O!
With a BAA BAA here

And a BAA BAA there
Here a BAA
There a BAA
Everywhere a BAA BAA
Old MacDonald had a farm
Ee-Yi-Ee-Yi-O!

Old MacDonald had a farm
Ee-Yi-Ee-Yi-O!
And on that farm he had a Dog
Ee-Yi-Ee-Yi-O!
With a WOOF WOOF here
And a WOOF WOOF there
Here a WOOF
There a WOOF
Everywhere a WOOF WOOF
Old MacDonald had a farm
Ee-Yi-Ee-Yi-O!

Old MacDonald had a farm
Ee-Yi-Ee-Yi-O!
And on that farm he had a Cat
Ee-Yi-Ee-Yi-O!
With a MIAOW MIAOW here
And a MIAOW MIAOW there
Here a MIAOW
There a MIAOW
Everywhere a MIAOW MIAOW
Old MacDonald had a farm
Ee-Yi-Ee-Yi-O!

Old MacDonald had a farm
Ee-Yi-Ee-Yi-O!
And on that farm he had some Cows
Ee-Yi-Ee-Yi-O!
With a MOO MOO here

And a MOO MOO there
Here a MOO
There a MOO
Everywhere a MOO MOO
Old MacDonald had a farm
Ee-Yi-Ee-Yi-O!

Old MacDonald had a farm
Ee-Yi-Ee-Yi-O!
And on that farm he had some Horses
Ee-Yi-Ee-Yi-O!
With a NEY NEY here

And a NEY NEY there
Here a NEY
There a NEY
Everywhere a NEY NEY
Old MacDonald had a farm
Ee-Yi-Ee-Yi-O!

Old MacDonald had a farm
Ee-Yi-Ee-Yi-O!
And on that farm he had
A Kangaroo, An Elephant, A Giraffe, A Hippopotamus,
A Bear, A Gorilla, A Tiger, and a Snake
Ee-Yi-Ee-Yi-O!

With a BOING ARROOO here
And a MUNCH FLOBBLE there
Here a GRRRR
There an AAK-AAK
Everywhere a ROOAARR SLITHER

Old MacDonald had a farm
Ee-Yi-Ee-Yi-O!

STICKER and COLOUR-IN PLAYBOOK

ANIMAL RHYMES

ILLUSTRATED BY
JENNY TULIP

I Love Little Pussy

I love little pussy,
Her coat is so warm,
And if I don't hurt her
She'll do me no harm.

She shall sit by my side,
And I'll give her some food;
And pussy will love me
Because I am good.

Pussy Cat, Pussy Cat

Pussy cat, pussy cat,
Where have you been?
I've been up to London
To visit the Queen.

Pussy cat, pussy cat,
What did you there?
I frightened a little mouse
Under her chair.

Baa, Baa, Black Sheep

Baa, baa, black sheep,
Have you any wool?
Yes, sir, yes, sir,
Three bags full;

One for the master,
And one for the dame,
And one for the little boy
Who lives down the lane.

Ride a Cock-Horse

Ride a cock-horse to Banbury Cross,
To see a fine lady upon a white horse;
Rings on her fingers and bells on her toes,
And she shall have music wherever she goes.

My Black Hen

Hickety, pickety, my black hen,
She lays eggs for gentlemen;

Gentlemen come every day
To see what my black hen doth lay.

Old Mother Hubbard

Old Mother Hubbard
Went to the cupboard,
To fetch her poor dog a bone;

But when she got there
The cupboard was bare
And so the poor dog had none.

This Little Pig

This little pig went to market.
This little pig stayed at home.

This little pig ate roast beef.
This little pig had none.

And this little pig went
SQUEAK SQUEAK SQUEAK
All the way home . . .

Goosie Goosie Gander

Goosie, goosie gander
Where shall I wander?
Upstairs and downstairs
And in my lady's chamber.

There I met an old man
Who would not say his prayers,
So I took him by the left leg
And threw him down the stairs.

Little Bo-Peep

Little Bo-peep has lost her sheep,
And doesn't know where to find them;
Leave them alone, and they'll come home,
Bringing their tails behind them.

Little Bo-peep fell fast asleep,
And dreamt she heard them bleating;
But when she awoke she found it a joke,
For they were still a-fleeting.

Then up she took her little crook,
Determined for to find them;
She found them indeed, but it made her heart bleed,
For they'd left their tails behind them.

It happened one day, as Bo-peep did stray
Into a meadow close by,
That there she espied their tails
    side by side,
All hung on a tree to dry.

She heaved a sigh, and wiped her eye,
And over the hillocks went rambling,
And tried what she could, as a
    shepherdess should,
To pin back each tail to its lambkin.

Three Little Kittens

Three little kittens
They lost their mittens,
And they began to cry,
Oh, mother dear,
We sadly fear
Our mittens we have lost.
What! Lost your mittens,
You naughty kittens!
Then you shall have no pie.
Mee-ow, mee-ow, mee-ow.
No, you shall have no pie.

The three little kittens
They found their mittens,
And they began to cry,
Oh, mother dear,
See here, see here,
Our mittens we have found.
Put on your mittens,
You silly kittens,
And you shall have some pie.
Purr-r, purr-r, purr-r,
Oh, let us have some pie.

Hey Diddle Diddle

Hey diddle, diddle,
The cat and the fiddle,
The cow jumped over the moon;
The little dog laughed
To see such fun,
And the dish ran away with the spoon.

Mary had a Little Lamb

Mary had a little lamb,
Its fleece was white as snow;
And everywhere that Mary went
The lamb was sure to go.

It followed her to school one day,
That was against the rule;
It made the children laugh and play
To see a lamb at school.

Three Blind Mice

Three blind mice, three blind mice,
See how they run, see how they run!
They all ran after the farmer's wife,
Who cut off their tails with a carving knife,
Did you ever see such a thing in your life,
As three blind mice?

STICKER and COLOUR-IN PLAYBOOK

NURSERY RHYMES

ILLUSTRATED BY
JENNY TULIP

Hush-a-Bye Baby

Hush-a-bye baby, on the tree top,
When the wind blows the cradle will rock;

When the bough breaks the cradle will fall
Down will come baby, cradle and all.

Humpty Dumpty

Humpty Dumpty sat on a wall,
Humpty Dumpty had a great fall;

All the King's horses and all the King's men
Couldn't put Humpty together again.

Little Jack Horner

Little Jack Horner
Sat in the corner,
Eating a Christmas pie;

He put in his thumb,
And pulled out a plum,
And said, What a good boy am I!

Little Miss Muffet

Little Miss Muffet
Sat on a tuffet,
Eating her curds and whey;

There came a big spider,
Who sat down beside her
And frightened Miss Muffet away.

37

Simple Simon

Simple Simon met a pieman,
Going to the fair;
Says Simple Simon to the pieman,
Let me taste your ware.

Says the pieman to Simple Simon,
Show me first your penny;
Says Simple Simon to the pieman,
Indeed I have not any.

Pat-a-Cake, Pat-a-Cake

Pat-a-cake, pat-a-cake, baker's man,
Bake me a cake as fast as you can;

Pat it and prick it, and mark it with T,
And put it in the oven for Tommy and me.

Georgie Porgie

Georgie Porgie, pudding and pie,
Kissed the girls and made them cry;

When the boys came out to play,
Georgie Porgie ran away.

The Old Woman in a Shoe

There was an old woman who lived in a shoe,
She had so many children she didn't know what to do;

She gave them some broth without any bread;
Then she whipped them all soundly and put them to bed.

Tom, The Piper's Son

Tom, Tom, the piper's son,
Stole a pig and away he run;

The pig was eat,
And Tom was beat,
And Tom went howling down the street.

Jack be Nimble

Jack be nimble,
Jack be quick,
Jack jump over
The candlestick.

Sing a Song of Sixpence

Sing a song of sixpence
A pocket full of rye;
Four and twenty blackbirds,
Baked in a pie.

When the pie was opened,
The birds began to sing;
Now wasn't that a pretty dish,
To set before the King?

The King was in his counting house,
Counting out his money;
The Queen was in the parlour,
Eating bread and honey.

The maid was in the garden,
Hanging out the clothes,
When down came a blackbird
And pecked off her nose.

They sent for the King's doctor,
Who sewed it on again,
And he sewed it on so neatly,
The seam was never seen.

Little Boy Blue

Little Boy Blue,
Come blow on your horn,
The sheep's in the meadow,
The cow's in the corn.

Where is the boy
Who looks after the sheep?
He's under the haystack
Fast asleep.
Will you wake him?
No, not I,
For if I do,
He's sure to cry.

Jack and Jill went up the Hill

Jack and Jill
Went up the hill,
To fetch a pail of water;
Jack fell down,
And broke his crown,
And Jill came tumbling after.

Contrary Mary

Mary, Mary, quite contrary,
How does your garden grow?
With silver bells and cockle shells,
And pretty maids all in a row.

STICKER and COLOUR-IN PLAYBOOK

THE TEDDY BEAR DANCE

ILLUSTRATED BY
JENNY TULIP

When the night is fresh and the air is clear
When owls hide their eyes and fireflies appear
Then Teddy Bear Time is here
There are Teddy Bears dancing here!

Out from the beds of their daytime chums
Silently drawn by the beat of the drums
From every house in the town they come
The little bears all intent on fun

In a moonlit dale in the dead of night
The teddies arrive at their secret site
Once a year on this very same date
They gather together to celebrate

A wonderful table is laid for a treat
A feast of cakes and jellies to eat
Balloons and crackers and nuts to wear
And brightly wrapped presents for every bear

53

All kinds of bears are here at the ball
Fat ones and thin ones, large ones and small
Bears with waistcoats, canes and spats
Bears with tee-shirts and silly sun-hats

Teddies from Persia, Peking and Peru
From Texas, Tibet and Timbuctoo
Teddies from Russia, Spain and France
Every bear nation has come to the dance

The Teddy Bear king and his beautiful queen
Stand on their thrones to be easily seen
The king lifts his paw, a prearranged sign
That it is now formally Teddy Bear Time

Magical notes drift into the air
Wonderful music is heard everywhere
The teddy band strikes up a wild dancing beat
And the bears begin to stamp with their feet

The teddies start dancing in pairs and in teams
Spinning so fast they are bursting their seams
Twirling the tango, the reel and quadrille
Each bear is dancing as hard as he will

The teddies dance out through cities and towns
They dance over hills and valleys and downs
They dance so fast and so quick and so high
That soon they are dancing aloft in the sky

The teddy dance rises up over the trees
And then over mountains, rivers and seas
It flies over castles with turreted towers
It flies over meadows covered in flowers

Further and further the teddies dance
Higher and higher they twirl and prance
Up through the clouds to the stars and the moon
They dance through the skies to the heavenly tune

In a far-away glimmer the dawn starts to rise
The teddy king laughs and says "my how time flies!"
The band slows the tune to the gentlest sound
And the little bears float softly down to the ground

Knowing it's late and they must get home soon
While the spell still holds by the light of the moon
Every bear scampers home and pops into its bed
Where sleep quickly covers up each tired-out ted

As dawn breaks the children awake from their sleep
But from their teddies there comes not a peep:
Just slumbering soft, such a sweet light sight
As if they'd been there the whole of the night!

pages 2–3

pages 4–5

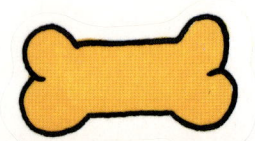

pages 6–7

pages 8–9

pages 10–11

pages 12–13

pages 14–15

page 16

pages 18–19

pages 20–21

pages 22–23

pages 24–25

pages 26–27

pages 28–29

pages 30–31

page 32

pages 34–35

pages 36–37

pages 38–39

pages 40–41

pages 42–43

pages 44–45

pages 46–47

page 48

pages 50–51

pages 52–53

pages 54–55

pages 56–57

pages 58–59

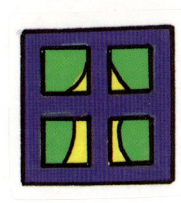

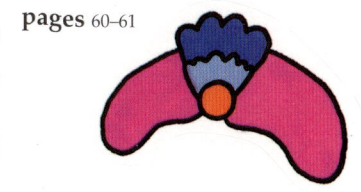

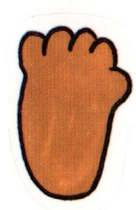

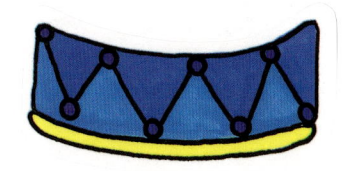

pages 60–61

pages 62–63

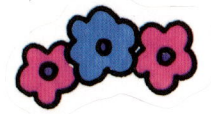

page 64